Presented by

THE BIRCH FAMILY AND FRIENDS

IN MEMORY OF

WILLIAM "BILL" BIRCH

2004

RACE CAR LEGENDS

CHELSEA HOUSE PUBLISHERS

OFF-ROAD RACING

Sue Mead

CHELSEA HOUSE PUBLISHERS
Philadelphia

Frontis: *The thrill and adventure of off-road racing draws hundreds of enthusiasts to this popular motorsport. A four-wheel drive vehicle, like the Land Rover in this picture, can take on the most rugged of terrain.*

Produced by
21st Century Publishing and Communications, Inc.
New York, New York
http://www.21cpc.com

CHELSEA HOUSE PUBLISHERS

Production Manager: Pamela Loos
Art Director: Sara Davis
Director of Photography: Judy L. Hasday
Managing Editor: James D. Gallagher
Senior Production Editor: J. Christopher Higgins
Publishing Coordinator/Project Editor: James McAvoy

The Chelsea House World Wide Web address is
http://www.chelseahouse.com

First Printing

1 3 5 7 9 8 6 4 2

Library of Congress Cataloging-in-Publication Data

Mead, Sue.
  Off road racing: legends and adventures / Sue Mead.
    p.   cm.—(Race car legends)
  Includes bibliographical references.
  ISBN 0-7910-5851-4
  1. Off-road racing—Juvenile literature. 2. Automobile racing drivers—Juvenile
literature. [1. Off-road racing. 2. Automobile racing drivers.] I. Title. II. Series.

GV1037.M43 2000
796.72—dc21
[B]   00-038404
                                                            CIP
                                                            AC

CONTENTS

DANGER AND DRAMA
ON THE DAKAR

It was day six of our off-road race across northern Africa, a route that would take us west to east from Dakar, Senegal, to the pyramids in Cairo, Egypt. For an entire day we had jounced and bounced our way more than 400 miles from the nation of Burkina, racing east to its neighbor Niger. The race challenged every bone, muscle, and brain cell in my body. It also challenged the mechanics, windscreen, and wheels of our race-prepared Kia Sportage sport utility vehicle (SUV).

For six days from the start of the race in Dakar, we had driven through a landscape that looked like the pictures from the pages of a 1950s *National Geographic* magazine. The landscape would abruptly change from terrain to terrain, and so did our race tactics. Heading east, we crossed Senegal's bushy savanna and wound our way over and through the twisty tracks and dense, tropical vegetation of Mali. Then it was the Sahel Desert and the fast, arid

A Kia Sportage sport utility vehicle lines up in Paris, France, ready for the famed Dakar 2000 race from Paris to Dakar to Cairo. Photojournalist, off-road enthusiast, and author Sue Mead was with racer Darren Skilton as navigator on this grueling 7,000-mile trek across the forbidding landscape of North Africa, and she recounts her experiences in this book.

stretches of Burkina to the sandy trails and pink dunes along the River Niger to our destination in Niamey, capital city of Niger.

It was in Niamey that we heard the bad news. We were stunned when the director of the rallye, Hubert Auriol, read us a message that would change the course of history for the famed Dakar race.

Auriol informed us that a group of more than 300 armed men, calling themselves the Islamic Dissident Army, was preparing to attack the rallye with 40 vehicles and a store of heavy weapons. There was complete silence from the assembled group of competitors and press from 31 countries around the globe, as we stood on the tarmac of the Niamey airbase in the steamy heat of the night. Generators that provided our electricity hummed against the darkness.

As a result of the threat, we decided to airlift our entire operation to Libya, the land of dictator and sometime supporter of terrorists, Mu'ammar Gadhafi. From the city of Sabha in central Libya, we would continue the Dakar race five days from now. It was clear that our situation was complicated and the solution costly.

Our race life soon took on the feel of a James Bond adventure when we learned that three Russian Antonovs, the world's largest aircraft, were on their way from Siberia to assist in our airlift to Libya. It seemed like something out of a *Mission: Impossible* script to move our rolling stock to Libya. There were more than 600 competitors on some 200 motorcycles and in 141 cars and 65 big trucks. There was also an entourage of race organizers, mechanics, medics, caterers, and the press. All in all, there were close to 1,500 people involved. We were

learning that off-road racing can sometimes present more dangers and difficulties than ordinary racing.

Since the famed Dakar rallye began in 1978, it has developed a lore that has captured the hearts of racers around the globe. The rallye has also grown to become one of the world's top five adventures (climbing Mt. Everest in Nepal claims the top spot). The millennium edition and 22nd annual running of this rigorous race seemed a challenging and arduous task even

One of the several helicopters that accompanied the Dakar race is loaded into an aircraft at the Niamey airport. Because of terrorist threats, the expedition could not cross much of the Sahara Desert, so people and machines had to be flown to Libya instead. The airlift of some 400 vehicles and more than 1,000 people cost more than $4 million.

before we experienced the threat of terrorists in the middle of the route—a route of nearly 7,000 miles that was new and unique.

The first Dakar rallye followed a 6,200-mile-long route from Paris to Algiers, in Algeria, to Dakar. It was organized in 1978 by Thierry Sabines, a successful European rallye racer, after he had ridden a Yamaha XT500 in an off-road race from Abidjan on Africa's Ivory Coast to Nice, France. The first Dakar drew 90 motorcycles and 80 cars to the competition. Of the 170 entries, only 74 crossed the finish line, with one death and a series of disasters. Medical teams traveled in two-wheel drive Peugeot 504s.

Sabines's focus was on human adventure. He wanted man to go beyond his known limits to overcome the worst adversities and challenges that could arise from trying to reach Dakar from Paris. With only a basic road book, a map, and a compass, racers drove what were essentially stock vehicles. They ate military rations and didn't shower for a full two weeks.

While much remains the same 22 years later, the magnitude of the race and its logistics have changed. The Dakar 2000 saw 404 entries at the symbolic start, near the Eiffel Tower in Paris. Following the fanfare, vehicles were boated to Africa and contestants were flown to the official start of the race in Dakar. After 18 days, 107 motorcycles, 96 cars, and 5 trucks crossed the podium in front of the pyramids in Cairo. Year 2000's event employed 22 aircraft, 8 helicopters, and 39 organizer trucks (including medical and television vehicles). Close to 1,500 people, including competitors, airborne mechanics, organizers, journalists, and doctors, followed the rallye and camped out each night. Catering needs for this entourage were met by 6 trucks, 153 tons of food, and a mobile kitchen with 12 ovens.

I am a motor journalist who specializes in four-wheel drive vehicles (4WDs) and off-road adventures. I was very familiar with the Dakar race when Darren Skilton of Baja Automotive Adventures called nearly a year prior to the 2000 event and asked me to join him as copilot. Skilton is a two-time Short Course Off-Road Enthusiasts (SCORE) Class 3 desert-racing champion. (Class 3 is for short-wheelbase, four-wheel drive sport utility vehicles.) I had already raced with him once and had found him talented, amiable, and fluent in three languages—a useful skill in international racing. Skilton had been racing for Kia Motorsports for about three years and was already very experienced in international rallyes.

Having taken part in many previous expeditions, I had a great deal of racing experience. My races included four Camel Trophies, three record-setting drives, two Baja 1000s, and Nevada's Laughlin Desert Series Primm 300, which was the first off-road race in which I was sitting behind the wheel. However, none of them could totally prepare me for the Dakar 2000.

If you don't like the dust or heat, you wouldn't have come to Africa, Hubert Auriol pointed out at the drivers' meeting the night before the start of the race. It was simply understood that if you could not accept the challenges, you would not have joined the trek across North Africa. There would be long, hard days, short, hard nights, and a competition schedule that was like racing 17 back-to-back Baja 500s (a grueling event in Mexico's peninsula of Baja California).

The night before the race started, I suddenly took stock of the extent of this adventure. I know that racing is dangerous. During that day, however, while attending a series of required sessions, I realized its lengthy list of hazards. We were briefed on such topics as how to set off the distress beacon, what to do when you were lost or broken down off of the main track (wait 24 hours before setting off the distress beacon), and how much water and salt to consume every day (more than you would imagine). I also learned that three competitors had died of dehydration the year before. I immediately began to drink liquids.

In addition, I was awed by our Class T3.3 competition (which included the Renault buggy driven by the overall race winner, Jean-Louis Schlesser). Our team had believed that the Kias would be ranked in the far less competitive T3.1 category. The judges thought differently, though. They considered the cars to be SCORE vehicles, and no amount of protesting would change their call. Our goal and that of Kia Motors America was for us and their two Korean-built, 150-horsepowered Sportages simply to finish. Being ranked in the T3.1 class made it clear that we would eat dust.

The airlift meant that we would race only 13 days over some 5,000 miles, missing out on the treacherous Tenere Desert. The Dakar would have the highest percentage of finishers ever. Despite hardships, horsepower, and terrorists,

the two Kia teams would see amazing sights—a volcano that contained an oasis and a lake. We would successfully navigate hundreds of miles of dunes and descend 160-foot-high cliffs in the Great Sand Sea of the Sahara Desert. And we would arrive safely at the finish—the base of the pyramids in Cairo.

Crossing the podium in Cairo with Skilton, I remembered the advice that 19-year Dakar veteran and Mitsubishi mechanic Ulrich Bremmer had given to me early in the race: First, you must fight Africa; second, you must fight yourself; then, you can fight the competition.

The thrill of finishing the Dakar is evident in the faces of the U.S. team perched on their vehicles at the foot of the pyramids in Cairo. Driver Curt LeDuc and navigator Pepe Martinez are at left. Skilton (right) puts his arm around a smiling Mead (to his right). The two Kias finished in 41st and 56th place, putting them in the top 40 percent of their class. Only 96 of the original 141 cars finished the race.

PREPARING FOR THE DAKAR

Being ready for a race the magnitude of the Dakar 2000 takes many months of preparation and training for the team as well as many months of work and testing on the cars. Participating in other races becomes a proving ground, and my first race with Darren Skilton was exactly that. We both learned a lot.

Skilton, 33, spent his childhood working with his father, also a race car driver. By 1991, he began his motorsports career in earnest by navigating for legendary off-road champion Don Adams in the Baja 1000. In 1992, after graduating from Cal State Fullerton with a B.A. degree in political science, Darren began driving in desert races. He won the Baja 100 twice and captured three class championships. In 1995, he began racing internationally, becoming the only American driver ranked for the Federation of International Automobiles (FIA) Cross-Country Rallies. Skilton competed in races including the Atlas

Darren Skilton (right), posing here with author Sue Mead and their Kia Sportage, asked Mead to partner with him in the Dakar 2000. To prepare, Mead spent months training and driving. Her experiences in prep races, such as Nevada's Primm 300, helped her hone her skills and develop the endurance needed for the Dakar.

Rallye in Morocco, Baja Portugal, and Baja España. He was the 1999 champion of the SCORE series in Class 3.

Our race was the last of a four-race series in the Best in the Desert competition for the 1998 season. We were challenging the Nevada desert in the Terrible's Town 250, known as the richest off-road race in Nevada. It wasn't just the purse that Skilton was chasing, however. Although simply starting the race would give him the points he needed to clinch a class win in this series, Skilton's goal was to finish the race.

With only six years in competition, Skilton had already garnered three SCORE Milestone Awards for finishing every mile of every race he started. He had also gained significant wins, including two SCORE Baja 1000 titles. But the 1998 season was plaguing him like a competitor he just couldn't get past.

We started the Terrible's Town at Pahrump, Nevada. Encased in our Kia Sportage, we were jouncing along when suddenly 3,350 pounds of sheet metal came to a jarring halt. "She died on that last bump," Skilton yelled into my radioed helmet. "Radio [Crew Chief] Barrie Thompson and tell him where we are," Skilton directed. He undid his air hose and radio controls, threw off his five-point harness, and jumped out of the vehicle.

I had just seen mile marker 102, and we had passed Barrie Thompson only four miles before as we cleared pit #3, in Crater Flat. In fact, I had given a thumbs up, signaling all's well, as we powered by our pit crew at what was close to the halfway point of the race.

Skilton tore off the hood and threw it on the dry scrub. The problem was quickly revealed. A

Three-time Class 3 SCORE champion Darren Skilton drives the Kia Sportage for Kia Motors America. He is one of the greats in desert racing and has driven in most of the best-known off-road events, including the Baja 1000.

fitting in the fuel line leading to the manifold had loosened. "Hold this and let me know if fuel comes out," Skilton gestured.

A hopeful yes was soon followed by a sorry no. "We're out of fuel," said Skilton.

He had assumed that the 32-gallon fuel cell carried a 150-mile range that would see us through to pit #4 at mile 137. His math was correct, but he had not accounted for the slow drip of fuel onto the sand track that began at some point after our start. In addition, he had not figured for the condition of the course. Some 150 motorcyles, quads, buggies, and

Drivers and vehicles get ready at the starting line of the Terrible's Town 250 in Pahrump, Nevada, in December 1998. Mead accompanied Skilton on the race, which was disastrous after their Kia broke down.

trucks had made mashed-potato, gas-guzzling goo out of the miles of soft silt along the track.

Not a soul was in sight as we stood shivering on the western edge of Death Valley. Any hardy racers that would soon be barreling along, leaving us in their dust cloud, would be racing to beat the clock to the next three pits and the finish line. It was easy to assume they would not be carrying extra fuel when every ounce in a race car counted.

Each minute lost was critical, and I had 65 of them to use. We radioed Thompson repeatedly to check on his luck in obtaining fuel, a fuel can, and then a racer who would be kind enough to make the drop.

At last fuel arrived in a cloud of dust, delivered by Truck 8008, which was powered by Brian Burns and Eddie Oddone of Sun Valley, California. Using a razor blade, we cut the ropes to the two five-gallon fuel cans. Hoisting the cans, as Burns and Oddone motored off, we poured gasoline into the fuel-filler opening, down the side of the Kia, and onto us.

Starting up again, we approached mile 113. This point had been a caution spot from the drivers' meeting the night before. We were warned of a steep, single-lane, downhill track with severe drop-offs. As we rounded the bend, our hearts steeled. Burns, Oddone, and their battered blue Ford truck were stopped in the track with a broken tie-rod. As we attempted to pass, Oddone remarked, "If you go over, it'll end your racing career."

We had to forget practice, preruns, driving talent, and the Kia's impressive engine, tires, and racing wheels. The Terrible's Town 250 was over.

Following this race, Skilton and I strapped ourselves into the Sportage again for two races as a part of our training program for the Dakar. We also went to the Dumont Dunes Off-Road Vehicle Area near Death Valley, California. The terrain there is very similar to what we would experience in the African deserts. At Dumont Dunes, we checked out the Kia, the tires, and various tire pressures and worked on our technique and equipment for becoming unstuck in sand.

First, however, we had to become stuck. It was not as easy as we thought because the Kia and its tires worked very well in the sand. Once we were stuck, we did learn that our sand tracks accomplished the job. They provided a ramp for the tires to climb out of the sand, but we needed something to scoop sand from under the belly of the SUV. Skilton went back to his shop and designed a long metal rake with a scooped end that we used on the Dakar.

Both of our shakedowns for the Dakar were SCORE events. The 1999 Laughlin/SCORE Desert Series Primm 300 in Nevada became the training ground for me to get behind the wheel and drive. I drove one of the three 87-mile laps, and it was a thrill when we won our class.

Our next race was the 1999 Baja 1000, whose course is more than twice the distance of the Primm 300. In this race, Skilton was behind the wheel with Curt LeDuc, whose unusual talent as both driver and engineer has made him a hot commodity on the international scene. I practiced navigating as well as honing the physical and mental endurance skills I would need on the Dakar.

Having Curt LeDuc as codriver was a big plus. Beginning in 1975, LeDuc had raced in off-road events in his native Massachusetts before relocating to southern California. He has designed, manufactured, and maintained race vehicles as well as becoming a skilled driver. Jeep, Kia, Ford, Chevrolet, and Dodge have used his expertise in constructing race cars and trucks. LeDuc's racing highlights include becoming the 1994 Short Course Off-Road Driver's Association (SODA) world champion, overall winner in the 1995 Baja 500, champion in the 1997 SCORE Trophy Truck series, and the 1999 Pike's Peak Rookie of the Year.

With both Skilton and LeDuc behind the wheel, the Kia Sportage finished the Baja course in 21 hours and 21 minutes. It was a

great victory for Skilton, who clinched the 1999 SCORE Class 3 championship with this win.

While there was nothing we did that could truly prepare us for the Dakar, it is clear that *everything* we did prepared us for it. But we would learn, like everyone who participates in off-road racing and other motorsports events, that some days you run out of gas, sometimes you win, and sometimes simply to finish is to win.

Breaking down in desert sands is not a new experience for off-roaders. Often, drivers have to "winch" their vehicles, as racer Tom Collins is preparing to do here. A winch is a machine with wire cables that hauls a stuck vehicle out of sand or mud.

How It All Began

Off-road racing can trace its roots back to 1909, when Erwin "Cannonball" Baker traveled to Indianapolis to visit the city's new motor speedway. After winning a 10-mile race on his Indian-brand motorcycle, he signed a contract with the manufacturer and made a series of cross-country runs promoting these bikes. As automobiles became more popular, Baker earned other sponsorships from manufacturers and drove their vehicles cross-country as well. Baker got his nickname from an enthusiastic newsman who wrote, "He came across like a cannonball" when the reporter saw the rider blast across the finish line on a coast-to-coast run. As there were only a handful of paved roads during Cannonball's day, many consider him the country's first off-road racer.

Like the World Series in baseball and the Super Bowl for football, the Baja 1000 has become the

Pictured to the left is a Hummer four-door wagon at a recent Baja 1000 off-road race. The greatest test of endurance for both driver and vehicle in off-road racing is the Baja 1000, run through Mexico's Baja peninsula. Often called the "roughest run under the sun," the competition, organized in 1967, draws scores of drivers and vehicles and hundreds of enthusiasts and has helped make off-road racing a major motorsport.

ultimate competition for the breed of racer that Cannonball Baker inspired. Since 1967, the giants of off-road racing have gathered in Mexico's Baja California to race against themselves and the clock.

The traditional drive is from Tijuana (just south of the U.S. border) to La Paz, at the tip of the peninsula. The Baja desert gets very little rainfall and is so dry that dust is one of the major challenges facing the drivers. Baja is a mostly barren and largely empty place—perfect for long off-road races. It is no wonder that competing at the Baja is clearly considered the most challenging and alluring event in American off-road racing.

It was not until 1962—more than 50 years after Cannonball Baker's famous high-speed runs—that anyone raced in Baja. That year, Dave Ekins and Bill Robertson Jr. sped from Tijuana to La Paz on a pair of Honda 250 motorcycles. They made the 950-mile trip on a whim. Because there were no official timers, the riders carried sheets of paper and had them stamped at the telegraph offices in each town. Ekins made the run in 39 hours, 54 minutes. Robertson came in less than an hour later. The Baja had entered the record books.

That same year, General Motors' Chevrolet division commissioned a handful of custom-built trucks for a run from Long Beach, California, to La Paz. Even though the trucks were not especially fast, the run garnered valuable publicity for the automaker. It also introduced a new segment of off-road desert racing as well. Advertisements of the period billed the Baja the "roughest run under the sun."

During the next four years, motorcyclists tried

to beat Dave Ekins's 1962 record but failed. In 1966, Dave made the run again with his brother Bud, Eddie Mulder, and Cliff Coleman. This time the quartet rode far more powerful Triumph 500 and 650 motorcycles. Still, they only bettered the 1962 time by eight minutes! Part of the delay was a 10-minute search for the telegraph office in La Paz; it had been moved since Ekins's last visit. In any case, the 1962 record seemed hard to beat.

It is just this sort of "unbeatable" record that

The barren, forbidding terrain of the Baja wilderness is both an obstacle and a challenge to off-roaders. Since racers first began confronting it in the 1960s, what is now known as the Baja 1000 run has drawn scores of enthusiasts from around the world and has helped create many legendary race drivers.

has drawn the fastest and most daring racers out of their workshops. In late 1966, John Crean and John Cummings made the first high-speed dune buggy run of the 1000. Their custom Meyers Manx buggies were derived from the Volkswagen Beetle and sported four-wheel drive and long-travel suspension. Their total elapsed time was 89 hours, 23 minutes.

Crean and Cummings's time was a far cry from the 39-hour motorcycle record, but the idea of using a four-wheel drive vehicle would not go away. In April 1967, Ted Mangels and Bruce Meyers (the builder of the famous buggies) beat every established record with their 34-hour, 45-minute run from La Paz to Tijuana. Their time would have been an hour or two faster had the tourist office in Tijuana not been closed when they arrived. That office was their last stop, since it was the Mexico Department of Tourism that had certified the run.

Momentum to race what became known as "The Road" (when there really wasn't a road at all) was building quickly. The summer of 1967 saw two important Baja runs. In June, two Toyota Land Cruisers with powerful Chevrolet V-8 engines made the trip under the leadership of Ed Orr, Claude Dozier, Ed Pearlman, Dick Cepek, John Lawlor, and Drine Miller. Their 41-hour time was unremarkable and showed that Baja could not be won on horsepower and four-wheel drive alone.

The real shock to the off-road community came in July, when a lowly passenger car tackled the Tijuana-La Paz journey. Journalists Ralph Poole and Spencer Murray borrowed a 1967 Rambler American two-door from the American Motors Corporation. In this basic car, the duo

made the trip in an astonishing 31 hours flat, giving pause to motorcycle and truck enthusiasts alike.

By the fall of 1967, it was becoming clear that more organization would be needed to organize and coordinate the future runs and make them easier. Under the leadership of Ed Pearlman, off-road enthusiasts formed the National Off-Road Racing Association (NORRA) and established the Mexican 1000 (the original name of the Baja 1000). The first official race

Tearing up the track in a cloud of dust, Darren Skilton and his Kia Sportage head for the finish line in the Baja 1000. With its wide tires, sturdy undercarriage, and four-wheel drive, the Kia is well equipped to challenge the rough terrain of the Baja landscape.

began in Tijuana on October 31, 1967, with 68 entries.

By this time, however, the Mexican government had understandably grown tired of no-holds-barred racing through the populated Tijuana outskirts. Officials insisted that the trip from Tijuana to Ensenada, 60 miles south, be conducted at a ceremonial low speed. The change made it impossible to compare the old times (Tijuana-La Paz) to the new, shorter run. The 950-mile Mexican 1000 in November 1967 was won by Vic Wilson and Ted Mangles in a Meyers Manx. They had a very respectable time of 26 hours and 8 minutes. This historic run marks the beginning of a distinguished era of serious off-road motorsports competition.

Over the years the Mexican 1000 became known simply as the Baja 1000. With the exception of the legendary 1972 event, the Baja ran nearly the same course until 1993. In the 1972 run, NORRA set the start in Mexicali, east of Tijuana on the Mexico-California border. The first half of the race coursed down the east coast of Baja through the the treacherous area called the Three Sisters. There, during practice trials, a group of racers including Parnelli Jones and Walker Evans were nearly swept to sea in a tropical storm.

After this race, NORRA lost control over the 1000. In 1973, seeking to tighten the reins on American dominance and to bring the event under local authority, Mexico transferred NORRA's permits to the Baja Sports Committee. This group of local business owners and officials lost thousands of dollars in the smaller Baja 500 in June of 1973. They decided not to hold the 1000 in 1974, in part because of the international fuel crisis that made motorsports extraordinarily expensive. Race cars are not known for their fuel efficiency.

Then, in 1975, the government of Baja California chose SCORE International to host the race. SCORE International was founded in 1972 by Mickey Thompson of Wilmington, California, who was called the "speed king." Many changes have occurred since Thompson dreamed of bringing off-road racing excitement to the masses, and his aide, Sal Fish, saw a major motorsport in the offing.

This recreational activity has grown into a sport with international prestige, a dedicated and fast-growing television audience, and even a home on the Internet. And SCORE has grown along with it, becoming the leading body in organizing and sanctioning off-road racing. SCORE is now most famous for its flagship event, the Baja 1000, which was recently renamed the Ford Tecate SCORE Baja 1000.

Beginning in 1975 and for four years, the Baja was run in a large loop beginning and ending at Ensenada. But in 1979 Mexican officials once again allowed competition on the Ensenada to La Paz route. Since then, the race has been run in a loop about half the time. In addition, Mexicali and Ojos Negros have also been designated as end points of the journey.

For 2000, however, a new Baja was in store. The racers were to begin at Ensenada and run nearly 2,000 miles by a circuitous route to San Lucas Cabo at the very tip of the peninsula. Times for the fastest vehicles were expected to be around 41 hours, with an overall time limit of 100 hours.

Whatever the route or the hazards, the Baja

Strapped into her seat, author Sue Mead poses with winning driver Rod Hall (right) at the 1999 Baja 1000. Each year, the Baja 1000 draws famous off-roading champions like Hall.

1000 attracts the best off-road racers from all corners of the globe. Participants hail from Argentina, Australia, Japan, Russia, Saudi Arabia, and from most of the nations in Europe. Mexico, Canada, and the United States are also well represented.

Some Baja greats began their careers in other motorsports. Parnelli Jones, Rick and Roger Mears, Danny Ongias, and Robby Gordon are heroes of the Indianapolis 500. Even drag racers have been lured to the unique challenge of Baja. Among the most famous off-roaders, though, are Rod Hall, Ron Bishop, Johny Johnson, and world motorcycle champions Malcolm Smith and Larry Roeseler. Hall and Bishop have competed in every SCORE Baja since its inception.

Although SCORE is by far the largest off-road racing body, some other organizations also further the sport. As well known as the SCORE Baja 1000 are the Best in the Desert Racing Association's series of runs. These, too, are huge events with extensive corporate sponsorship and more than 100 entries per race. Other organizations are for amateur racers, who typically start their careers in one of some dozen smaller groups. These groups host weekend races for cars, trucks, and motorcycles. Although the prizes are small, so are the entry fees, and the races usually have several dozen competitors.

Some of the better-known racing clubs include Mojave Desert Racing, Championship Off-Road Racing (CORR), Northern California and Nevada's Valley Off-Road Racing Association (VORRA), and the Southern Nevada Off-Road Enthusiasts (SNORE).

OFF-ROADING
IN THE JUNGLE

I lay U-shaped in a hammock with the oppressive tropical heat and humidity of Guatemala blanketing my aching body. The sun had set behind Lake Isabel's hills a couple of hours earlier, but its 127-degree wrath was still with us. Now, holding still for the first time in 17 hours, I was even more aware of my throbbing feet. They were stinging from an encounter with a mass of fire ants earlier in the day and sore from walking a good portion of the Spanish Track.

Where we were now, some 450 years earlier the Spanish adventurer Hernán Cortés and his conquistadors had laid a stone path on their march through the rain forest to the sea. That day, we inched our 33-vehicle convoy along the heavily overgrown, deeply rutted track. Teams armed with pickaxes, shovels, and chain saws cleared the way ahead.

It was Day 12 off-road in Central America, and I had finally grown used to the night sounds of the jungle. Howler monkeys screeched, winged things

Forging their way through nearly impassable jungles is one of the challenges that off-roaders love to tackle. Here, "Father of Four Wheeling" Mark A. Smith directs the movement of his Jeep through the trees and undergrowth of the treacherous Darien Gap in Central America. On average, the expedition traveled two or three miles a day.

cried and cawed, and a variety of animals that make the tropics their homes set up a symphony of sounds. It was the creatures that did not utter sounds—the venomous snakes, scorpions, tarantulas, and the dreaded centipedes—that I feared. They lived above and below the rain forest floor. I slept between their habitats.

We would be awakened when it was still dark, but it would be morning. Days were becoming a blur, and the clock, which ran on military time, didn't matter. We had to navigate more than 1,000 bone-jarring miles in 21 days, no matter what the conditions or the time. A couple of our team members had been airlifted out; many were being treated by the two physicians on our convoy. But the "Discos," as we affectionately called our diesel-fueled Special Edition Land Rover Discoverys, were running strong.

It all began in Grand Junction, Colorado, in a midwinter snowstorm. "Be careful what you wish for: it might come true!" cautioned Bill Baker as he offered me a handshake of congratulations. Baker, vice president of the Land Rover company, had just announced that I had been selected as the first female journalist from the United States to cover the world's most arduous four-wheel drive adventure—the Camel Trophy.

This had been my dream for four years, even though women were not accepted as applicants until 1994. Then, when I had applied, I was told I had to wait one more year to attend the U.S. trials in Colorado. There, in February, I joined 12 "bionics," as I respectfully called the men and women selected to try out for the competitive positions on the team.

Tom Collins, a veteran participant in the Camel Trophy, is the U.S. team coordinator.

Along with his staff, Collins provides a high level of training and support for the U.S. team through a series of practice weekends in Grand Junction. Then, at the International Trials and Training, Land Rover driving instructors and mechanics and the Camel Trophy management staff provide further instruction and rigorous training prior to the event.

The tryouts in Grand Junction comprised 30-hour, nonstop events in snow, sleet, and hail. Included were running, swimming, rope climbing, and map and compass tests. We were also exposed to knot tying, competitive driving, orienteering (cross-country racing using a map and compass), winching (using a machine to

Sue Mead (right) watches as Tom Collins (center), off-road legend and veteran participant in the Camel Trophy, inspects a tire during the 1997 Camel Trophy Expedition in Mongolia. Collins has competed around the globe. He was also in charge of Mead's training as she prepared for her first Camel Trophy race.

hoist a vehicle off the ground), and mechanics. It was a surprise to many, including me, that I finished. It soon became clear, though, that this was just the beginning.

Off-road racing and extreme four-wheeling adventure have much in common with other forms of racing or competition, but they also bring a unique set of challenges and training needs. Like other styles of racing, participants need to have a high level of physical and mental fitness along with the drive to win or succeed in their goals. But off-road events take place away from the pit crews and support teams of traditional racetracks. Because of this, off-road contestants must have the ability to fix their vehicles and endure the rigors of the deserts, jungles, mountains, or backcountry. They must also work as a team.

The Camel Trophy, called the Olympics of Four-Wheel Drive, is an extreme test of human and machine. Participants are required to learn skills that will help them survive the rigors of the race. Although still little-known in the United States, the Camel Trophy is a unique 4WD event that has brought great prestige to Land Rover vehicles and to race participants.

It all began in 1980, when three West German teams driving Jeep vehicles traversed the Transamizonica highway in Brazil's Amazon Basin. Known as the Highway of Tears, the 1,000 mile, 12-day journey was a daunting challenge through mud and harsh conditions that won the teams a hero's welcome upon their return.

Since 1981, Land Rover vehicles have been used in competitions that have been held in locations from Sumatra and Papua, New Guinea, to South America's Amazon region, to

Land Rovers are the vehicles of choice for the Camel Trophy races. Sturdy and reliable, the British-made, 4WD Land Rover can overcome most any challenge or obstacle, including this one's plunge into a river in the 1996 race.

eastern Siberia. Each year, competitors seek out some of the world's most remote and unnavigable terrain. (All travel is on current or pre-existing trails and supports the environmental principle of "Tread Lightly.")

Over the years, the Camel Trophy has grown to attract more than a million applicants for this annual trek, now considered one of the greatest adventures on the planet. Synonymous with the Camel Trophy and 4WD adventure is the name

Tom Collins (right) and Jeff Watkin demonstrate the ability of the Range Rover to slog through mud and muck. Collins declares that no matter how bad a situation he gets into, he has always figured a way out.

Tom Collins. A native of California who has lived in Colorado for nearly three decades, Collins represented the United States in the 1987 Camel Trophy. He and team member Dan Floyd of Clovis, California, tied for first place in that year's grueling competition that slogged across 1,000 miles of mud and muck in Madagascar. "It was the first time anyone had ever driven across the island from north to south," Collins explains with great pride. For Collins, however, the real prize was what followed.

Not long after Madagascar, Collins proposed the Great Divide Expedition to the Land Rover North America firm. The event, undertaken in August 1989, was designed to show that great driving expeditions in remote areas of the United States were possible in stock Range Rovers with stock tires. The 1,000-mile 4WD trek crossed the Continental Divide 15 times, passing through 32 high mountain passes. This milestone event led to other Land Rover adventure drives, a Land Rover driving school, and, in 1990, Collins's appointment as the trainer of the U.S. team.

Four-wheeling was not new to the physically fit, 6' 2" off-road expert, who has an athletic background and a degree in conservation. "I started four-wheeling at the age of six in my dad's '43 Ford GPW," Collins offers. "In my early years, I spent a lot of time with my dad and his friends in four-wheel drive vehicles. Our neighborhood had a '58 Series II Land Rover and I thought it was cool." Motorcycling followed, and Collins figures that, from 1969 to 1987, he spent "more than a hundred days a year" off-roading in a variety of vehicles.

Collins, whose off-road mileage has likely lapped the globe many times over, has four-wheeled on every continent except Australia and Antarctica. "The best part of it all, for me," he says, "is working with the training team to bring in a new group each year and watch them get better and better. What I enjoy most is seeing them all come home as new people after the experience of the Camel Trophy."

The affable off-road guru can't think of a

situation he would call "worst stuck." As he recalls: "It's a hard concept for me, because what most people would think about as worst—like the jungles of Amazon or Borneo—I like. I've never been so hopelessly stuck that I've been unable to figure a way out. When things are really bad and it's 3 A.M., I go to bed. When I wake up in the morning, and when my mind's clear, there's always a way out. What's really exciting is, when it becomes hopeless, other members of the team come up with ideas and it becomes a team effort."

At 48, Collins still easily spends more than 100 days a year in the business of four-wheeling. "When I was in Borneo two years ago, I realized on Day 20 that I was pooped out physically for the first time in my life. It was tough to be 46 and look at 26-year-olds still going strong and realize that I was slowing down a little bit," says Collins.

Don't tell that to the team, which Collins recently trained for the high-altitude, first-ever winter event of the Camel Trophy. They will tell you that Collins and past competitor Ken Cameron spent three nonstop days with them in June skiing, snowboarding, building snow caves, and white-water rafting to prepare them for this year's multidisciplined challenge. And, in the still-frigid waters of the Colorado River, when their raft capsized, Collins was twice pulled into a sinkhole. He came up and first checked to see that the others were safe. Assured, he broke into a smile. It was just another day in the backcountry for a man whose legend and lore have grown large both in the United States and around the world.

If Tom Collins is the guru of off-road racing, Mark Smith is the father of four wheeling, one

Laden with titles and accolades, Mark A. Smith has participated in and promoted off-road racing around the world. With his vehicles of choice, Jeeps, Smith has launched some of the sport's most difficult and thrilling adventures.

of his many titles. He has also been called Mr. Jeep and the John Wayne of Jeeping. Now that this 4WD expert is in his 70s, the new title Silver Fox of Four-Wheeling has been added to the list. Smith does for a living what most others only do for a hobby: he four-wheels America's—and the world's—fantastic frontiers.

Before Smith joined the U.S. Marines, he had already fallen in love with the Jeep, which he first saw in a newsreel at the movies. Once in the service and behind the wheel of a real Jeep, he began a relationship with this incredible machine that has now lasted for more than 50 years.

The tropical forests of Central America were a test of strength and endurance when Smith and his team tackled the Darien Gap. Here the team struggles to get one of their Jeeps across a river after building a raft to float the vehicle.

In 1952, Smith and a small group of businessmen and friends got together to talk about a way to support the sagging economy of their area in northern California. The idea of a Jeep trip across the famed, rugged Rubicon Trail was born. One hundred and fifty-five "Jeepers" and 55 Jeeps made the first trip across the 22-mile boulder-strewn trail to Lake Tahoe, near the Nevada border.

The craze caught on, and today more than 200,000 Jeep enthusiasts have driven across the trail and attended Jeep Jamborees, now held throughout the country. The family-oriented 4WD outings begun by Smith are designed for all levels of expertise. Beginners and seasoned off-roaders participate and are given instructional guidance over trails that are rated on a scale from 1 to 10 for difficulty.

The Rubicon is a 10.

The two-day events are held in a variety of locations in America's backcountry, with destinations selected for scenic and historical value as well as 4WD trails. The Rubicon and the Jeep Jamborees are only part of the Mark Smith story.

"I was looking for something more exciting in an off-road adventure when the idea of a trip crossing the Darien Gap came up," explains the tall gentle giant. The dream started in 1965, when Smith began thinking about the possibilities of an adventure deep in the heart of the Darien rain forest between Panama and Colombia in Central America. Seven years later, a British Army group tackled the nearly inpenetrable gap in a successful crossing, an ordeal that took 100 days and 250 men.

"This made me envious of their accomplishments but it did nothing to dampen my desire to try," says Smith, whose office walls are adorned with photos from 4WD expeditions around the world. "In 1976, I made a first exploration trip to the Darien, along with some friends. We felt the odds were against us, but felt the desire and need to conquer this feat."

The Darien, a snake- and insect-infested forest, became an obsession for Smith. He again explored the gap and the Great Atrato Swamp in Colombia a year later. Soon after their return, Smith and his friend and colleague, Ken Collins, picked a group of men and ordered their Jeep CJ5s. "We worked the bugs out of them on the Rubicon Trail. You see, the Rubicon Trail and the Jeepers Jamboree had given us the background and experience to embark on one of the greatest 4WD adventures ever taken," Smith explained.

After 12 years of dreaming and three years of planning, the Expedicion de las Americas began in 1978. The five-month, 21,000-mile-long journey was to take Smith's group from the tip of South America to Prudhoe Bay, Alaska. Smith described the expedition. "The trip was a tremendous experience and gave us a wonderful feeling of accomplishment—especially crossing the Darien Gap. On an average day there, we would make two or three miles. One day, we worked for nine hours and only moved 500 feet."

The group had to literally live off the land while carving out a trail in the dense forests. According to Smith, they ate whatever they could find. "The catch of the day, which was caught, trapped, shot, or snared by Indian hunters who accompanied our group, included turkeys, alligator[s], scarlet macaws, iguana, and a large variety of fish, along with native fruits and vegetables."

Now on record, Smith's Darien Gap crossing covered a total of 110 miles through this primitive forest. It was completed in 30 days by 14 North Americans, 3 Colombians, and 25 Central Americans.

It's easy to see why Smith's credentials support his reputation as one of the foremost 4WD celebrities in the world. Today, he is a consultant to the Jeep Division of Daimler Chrysler Corporation and has designed and built the 4WD test facility at the Daimler Chrysler proving ground in Chelsea, Michigan. He has developed special training for the U.S. Army Special Forces and has built more than 60 4WD test and demonstration courses in the United States and around the globe. Smith is also a member of the Off-Road Hall of Fame and the Explorers Club of

A U.S. Army Special Forces Jeep demonstrates its ability to negotiate the roughest terrain. The Jeep is Mark A. Smith's vehicle of choice, and as a trainer for the army, he has specialized in conducting Jeep tests and demonstrating its durability.

New York. In 1986, the United Four Wheel Drive Association named him the Four Wheeler of the Decade.

In addition to supporting the Jeep Jamboree USA program, Smith continues to share his expertise around the world, conducting special 4WD training schools where he teaches safe, commonsense off-road driving techniques. It is estimated that he has trained more than 2,000 law enforcement officers from 20 different agencies, including police and sheriff's departments in California and throughout the United States. California's Department of Fish and Game and the U.S. Forest Service have also benefitted from his training.

RACING GREATS

Off-road racing attracts scores of enthusiasts and boasts any number of talented people who are involved in this fast-growing motorsport. Some, like Parnelli Jones, began their careers in other kinds of car racing. Others, like Rod Hall and Walker Evans, started with off-roading. There are also those like Sal Fish and Casey Folks, who have helped to organize and promote the sport.

Parnelli Jones is among the most famous of American automobile racers. His career in motorsports covers such diverse areas as dirt-track races, stock car events, open-wheel racing, hill climbs, and desert endurance tests. He has won nearly every major auto race in the United States, including the Indianapolis 500.

Jones began his career in 1952, when he competed in a stock car event at a small dirt track in California and set off a 40-year winning spree. As he moved

Off-road racing boasts many legendary figures, including one of the best-known American auto racers, Parnelli Jones, here (right) talking with fellow racer Roger Mears. Jones's career has included competition in almost every area of racing, including the famed Indianapolis 500 as well as off-roading.

up to midgets and sprint cars, he sometimes raced four and five times a week. Jones finally made his first big race at the famous mile-long paved oval in Milwaukee, Wisconsin, in 1960. A year later he was voted Co-Rookie of the Year. By 1963 Jones handily won the Indianapolis 500, becoming the first driver ever to break the elusive 150 mph barrier. During his seven years at the Indy, Jones led a total of 492 laps, close to twice that of any other driver during that period. He also won a total of six other Indy car races.

In the late '60s and '70s, Parnelli Jones turned his attention to off-road racing, winning the famous Pike's Peak Hill Climb and both the Baja 500 and the 1000. He and his partner, Vel Miletich, established one of the most successful racing teams in history, hiring a number of top guns, including Al Unser, Mario Andretti, and Joe Leonard. Jones's well-respected and innovative team won a total of 53 Indy car races and competed in every type of race from the Baja to world-class Formula One events around the globe. Jones's enthusiasm for all things motorized has made him a hero to drivers and fans across the racing world.

Want to know Rod Hall's secret to off-road racing success? "It's this simple," Hall says. "It's more important to keep your vehicle together during the race than it is to be the fastest." That philosophy helped Hall on his way to being one of the winningest drivers in the history of the sport.

Hall began his career in the late '50s, in a Jeep CJ5. At that time he had to drive from

California to New Mexico and Colorado to compete in organized semiprofessional 4WD races. Today, Hall holds the distinction of being one of the winners of the inaugural Baja 1000 in 1967 and the only driver to win the Baja 1000 overall in a 4WD vehicle in 1972. He has competed in every Baja 1000, with his most recent win coming at the 1999 event in a Stock Full AMG Hummer. Hall has also raced and finished the famed Dakar.

Hall's awards include more than a dozen SCORE/HDRA (High Desert Racing Association)

When Rod Hall won the 1999 Baja 1000, he drove the new Hummer four-door wagon, shown here with a smiling Hall. With a record as one of off-road racing's most consistent winners, Hall competes annually in the Baja 1000. He also promotes and organizes off-road events.

titles and hundreds of individual-class wins. Now, in addition to racing for AMG Hummer, Hall conducts driver schools and adventure trips throughout the world, organizes corporate 4WD events, and builds race vehicles.

Walker Evans retired in 1999 after more than three decades of off-road racing. Like many of his peers, Evans was lured to the adventure of the Baja in the late 1960s. Working as a carpenter by day and at a racing shop by night, he eventually earned a seat in an American Motors Corporation Rambler to race in the 1969 Baja 500. Although his 21-hour time was unremarkable, he was hooked on the sport. (In fact, Walker later ran the entire 1000 in fewer hours.)

In the 1970s, Evans began racing Bill Stroppe's custom Ford trucks at the Baja. In his first run of the 1000, he eclipsed the factory-backed Fords by more than two minutes—not bad for the third race of his lifetime. A long winning streak followed, after which Evans joined Parnelli Jones's Chevrolet team, an experience that taught him the ropes of the racing life.

Fame and fortune came in the late 1970s, when Walker Evans teamed with a Ford dealership in southern California and authorized a signature pickup model. The deal was worth $25,000, and with that sum he was able to open his own racing shop. With the help of sponsors Dodge and Goodyear, Evans won the 1979 Baja 1000, finishing before every motorcycle, buggy, or other truck. His win was immediately hailed as a milestone victory in off-road racing. Not only did Evans's impressive achievements continue through the 1990s, he also became a role

Legendary racer Walker Evans crawls his modified Chevrolet Blazer over the rocks. Evans's sponsor is the Goodyear tire company, and he showed off their tires in that company's Extreme Rock Crawling Championship Series in Phoenix, Arizona, in April 2000.

model for modern legends like Ivan Stewart and the next generation of off-road racers.

The success of SCORE in Baja is due in large part to the efforts of the legendary Sal Fish. He first raced the 1000 in 1970, without much success. He and his codriver suffered continuous mechanical setbacks until a broken transmission left them stranded. In a stroke of luck during the middle of the night, a passing mechanic towed them to safety. "We went faster on a tow rope then we had been going in the race!" Sal jokes, recalling the doomed trip. Only four years later, Fish took control of SCORE and became the primary administrative figure in Baja racing. Today he is chief executive officer of the successful Los Angeles-based motorsports organization.

In his nearly three decades with SCORE, Fish has expanded media coverage of the Baja 1000 and other SCORE races significantly, earning spots on Speedvision and other cable television networks. Securing key sponsorships, without which the Baja adventure might have faded into history, are also among Fish's impressive achievements. Most importantly, he has focused on safety, developing a fast-response medical team to handle emergencies in the remote Baja desert. Fish has also organized a safety advisory board and worked closely with tourism departments to ensure the goodwill of the residents of the Baja peninsula. Not only has the Baja 1000 grown, it has grown responsibly under the leadership of Sal Fish.

In the off-road races in the United States, the only organization that compares in size or importance to SCORE is the Nevada-based Best in the Desert series. Behind this young but growing association is an off-road legend named Casey Folks.

Folks began his career in the 1960s as a competitor and has raced in more than 30 epic events in the Baja and North Africa. As an enthusiast and adventurer, he was quick to help organize the Incas Rallye in Peru and helped an Italian adventure firm run another rallye in Nevada.

Over the past decade, Folks has concentrated on bringing first-class off-road racing to his home state of Nevada. He began in 1993 by coordinating a 1,900-mile motorcycle endurance race around the Silver State, beginning and ending in Las Vegas. After three successful runs, Folks expanded this race with a difficult 500-mile leg to Reno, creating what has become known as the longest off-road race in the United States. For the millennium, Folks was working on a spectacular 2,000-mile endurance race called the Nevada 2000.

Among the off-road motorcyclists, Malcolm Smith is one of the all-time greats. Smith is the winner of more gold medals in the International Six-Day Trials than any other American, and he has done equally well with cycles and buggies. In the Mexican 1000 and its successor, the Baja 1000, Smith's record includes five firsts and four seconds in class. He markets motorcycle accessories through Malcolm Smith Enterprises.

Other legendary off-roaders have turned their racing skills to creating off-road equipment and products. Dick Cepek began selling farm-implement tires out of his garage in the early '60s. Today, he operates a multimillion-dollar enterprise, dealing not only in tires but in all types of off-road and outdoor equipment. He also took part in some of the Tijuana-to-La Paz record runs in 1967 that led to the first Mexican 1000. He is, in the

Thanks to Malcolm Smith, off-road motorcycle racing has gained tremendous popularity. At home with both bikes and other off-road vehicles, Smith has "ridden the dirt" in scores of races and is a valued adviser to numerous off-road motorcycle enthusiasts.

words of his copyrighted product slogan, "Baja Proven."

Bruce Meyers created the Meyers Manx buggy, which inspired more than 100 imitators and has become the most copied vehicle in automotive history. In April 1967, he and Ted Mangels drove a Manx from La Paz to Tijuana in a record time of 34 hours and 45 minutes. Meyers also raced a Manx in the 1967 Mexican 1000. He drove another innovative design of his, the Tow'd (buggy/off-road vehicle), in the 1968 Stardust 711 and the Mexican 1000.

Bill Stroppe's great contribution is getting vehicles ready for others. He prepared Lincolns for the Mexican Road Race and took a fleet of Chevrolet trucks from Tijuana to La Paz in 1962. Stroppe also built off-road racing Broncos and Ford pickups for Larry Minor, Rodney Hall, actor James Garner, and Walker Evans. But he is probably best known for having ridden bravely as Parnelli Jones's codriver during most of Jones's greatest off-road triumphs.

NORRA Cofounder and President Ed Pearlman originated the whole concept of modern off-road racing, pitting motorcycles, buggies, 4 x 4s, and even stock cars and trucks against one another in lengthy contests of endurance. He conceived the Mexican 1000, the Stardust 711, the Baja 500, and the Parker Dam 500. Many say that without Pearlman the off-road sport as we know it would not exist.

WHAT'S NEXT?

What's next in the world of off-road motorsports and racing? Perhaps a 4WD high-performance motorboard, a truly unique form of radical recreation —a mechanized skateboard. Described by its designer, Glenn Anderson, as a roller-coaster ride taken side-on, the new in-your-face 4 x 4 motorboard is quite unlike anything on the planet.

According to Anderson, all you really need are quick reflexes, an appetite for speed, and a touch of insanity to ride this machine. It was recently unveiled during a contest in New Zealand and showed off its power with bumps, jumps, and an off-road course through the woods.

Utilizing an unorthodox patented transmission and steering mechanism, this hands-free extreme machine is propelled by a high-performance, mid-mounted power plant, runs on 11-inch balloon tires with factory 5-inch mag rims, and reaches speeds of up to 30 mph over rugged terrain. This is not your father's Buick.

What may be new and next in off-roading will no doubt include vehicles like this Chinook recreational vehicle. It is the first four-wheel drive motor home to participate in a long race. In April 2000, it was driven in the grueling Alcan 5000 from Washington State to Alaska.

Each hand-assembled, signature-class machine has been designed from aluminum for minimum weight and maximum strength. The motorboard uses sophisticated and high-quality mechanical technology that marries the style and freedom of board riding with the speed and exhilaration of a motorsport. It has a lightweight aluminum chassis and employs hydraulic disc brakes. Riders are integrated to the board by step-in snowboard bindings with a remote hand control. Underneath, oil-bathed transmission components are sealed well away from dirt and mud. Weighing in at 55 pounds, the motorboard is easily transported in a trunk or truck or can be hauled to the beach or the backcountry.

Anderson and his business partner, Antony Bush, believe that what they have dubbed the Nitro Dirtboard will be heralded as the latest thrill-sport sensation. Already on the drawing board are ways to individualize it, including a silencer for those who like a purring sound from their vehicle. Also available are a full range of parts as well as after-market accessories. Anderson also markets a full line of protective wear, including the company's soon-to-be-released specially designed protective Dirtsuit.

While four-wheeling and off-road racing have been popular for many years, these pursuits have recently started to attract the mainstream attention they have long deserved. Today, with the increasing popularity of sport utility vehicles (SUVs) and personal pickup trucks for everyday car buyers, along with the growing appreciation for the benefits of 4WD traction, many more enthusiasts are interested in getting farther into the backcountry.

The "light truck" market, which includes SUVs

The latest in motorsport thrills is Glenn Anderson's motorboard, shown here with Anderson aboard at a show in Atlanta, Georgia. Riders can rock and roll on this machine, using the same techniques and balance as they would on a regular skateboard.

and pickups, is the fastest growing segment of the automobile market in the United States today. Two years ago, people had only two dozen SUVs to choose from. Today there are close to twice that number, and it is expected that within the next two years this number will have increased by 50 percent again. In addition, many manufacturers, such as

Not so long ago, off-road racing was unheard of in the United States. Today, its popularity is soaring. American contestants like Gregg Thomas (left) and Dean Vergillo, waving in triumph after finishing the 1998 Camel Trophy, have helped popularize the sport, drawing hundreds of participants and fans.

Kia, Jeep, and Land Rover, see the value of investing money in off-road racing programs to prove the ruggedness and durability of their products.

What's next? More of the same with increased numbers of people taking to the backcountry and participating in four-wheeling adventures. There is increased media coverage of the sport, including print and television. And now, enthusiasts can indulge their passion for adventure and thrills with a 4WD motorized skateboard.

GLOSSARY

class	Category in which vehicles are grouped according to such qualifications as kind of vehicle, size of wheelbase, engine power, drive system, and other requirements that the sponsoring organization may determine.
copilot	Second driver in car who accompanies the main driver.
driver	The person named to be the operator of a vehicle in an event.
expedition racing	The toughest off-road racing (such as the Dakar and Camel Trophy) which last over days or weeks and thousands of miles.
four by four (4 x 4)	Description of a vehicle with four-wheel drive. The first number is the number of wheels; the second is the number of powered wheels.
four-wheel drive (4WD) vehicle	Vehicle in which the power from the engine goes to all four wheels.
Jeep	Four-wheel drive American vehicle first used by the U.S. Army and later adapted for everyday use and off-road racing.
Land Rover	British four-wheel drive vehicle, also for everyday use and off-road racing.
sport utility vehicle (SUV)	A car or truck that can be used for racing sports.
two-wheel drive vehicle	Vehicle in which the power goes to only two wheels, either front or back.
winch	Machine for hoisting a vehicle into the air. It has wire cables or rope that winds around a drum as the vehicle is lifted.

FURTHER READING

Delong, Brad. *4-Wheel Freedom: The Art of Off-Road Driving.* Boulder, CO: Paladin Press, 1996.

Dimbleby, Nick. *Off-Road Driving Techniques.* United Kingdom: Crowood Press, 1997.

Gorr, Eric. *Motocross and Off-Road Motorcycle Performance Handbook.* Osceola, WI: Motorbooks International, 1996.

Hibbard, Jeff, and Ron Sessions. *Baja Bugs and Buggies.* Tucson, AZ: Berkley Publishing Group, 1982.

Holmes, Martin. *Rally Navigation: Develop Winning Skills with Advice from the Experts.* Newbury Park, CA: Haynes Publications, 1997.

Jackson, Jack. *The Off-Road 4-Wheel Drive Book: Choosing, Using and Maintaining Go-Anywhere Vehicles*, 4th Edition. Newbury Park, CA: Haynes Publications, 1999.

Statham, Steve. *Jeep Color History.* Osceola, WI: Motorbooks International, 1999.

WEBSITES

www.score-international.com

www.bitd.com

www.dakar.com

www.off-road.com

www.motocross.com

www.jeepunpaved.com

www.landrover.com

www.kia.com

ABOUT THE AUTHOR

Sue Mead began her automotive career as a part-time freelance evaluator for *Four Wheeler* magazine in 1988. Today, she travels the globe test-driving cars and trucks and working as a photojournalist/feature writer for more than four dozen publications. Mead specializes in 4WD and has been an auto editor for CNN/fn. She has been a participating journalist on three Camel Trophy adventures and an attending journalist on the Camel Trophy 1998 in Tierra del Fuego, Argentina. Mead has also participated in three record-setting adventure drives: the Arctic Circle Challenge 1995, the Tip to Tip Challenge 1996, and the TransAmerica Challenge 1997, and has codriven for Rod Hall in the Baja 1000.

Mead recently completed her first book, *Monster Trucks and Tractors*, published by Chelsea House. She is a member of the International Motor Press Association, the New England Motor Press Association, and the North American Car and Truck of the Year Jury. She recently completed the world's longest and most difficult off-road race, the Paris-Dakar-Cairo 2000.

ACKNOWLEDGMENTS

Special thanks to my two assistants, Ted Grozier, who helped with the research, writing, and editing of this book, and Tara McKay, who helped with typing.

Other thanks to Mark A. Smith, Tom Collins, Rod Hall, Parnelli Jones, Spencer Murray, Sal Fish, Casey Folks, and Deke Engel.

INDEX